THE WORLD OF THE
WOLF

Wolf in repose.

VICTORIA HURST, FIRST LIGHT

OVERLEAF: *Wolf song.*

DANIEL J. COX

THE WORLD OF THE
WOLF

C A N D A C E   S A V A G E

Sierra Club Books
San Francisco

Text copyright © 1996 by Candace Savage
Photographs copyright © 1996 by photographers credited
Originally published by Greystone Books, a division of Douglas & McIntyre Ltd.,
1615 Venables Street, Vancouver, British Columbia.

LIBRARY OF CONGRESS CATALOGING-IN-PUBLICATION DATA

Savage, Candace Sherk, 1949–
    World of the wolf / by Candace Savage.
      p.   cm.
    Rev. ed. of: Wolves. © 1988.
    Includes bibliographical references (p.   ) and index.
    ISBN 0-87156-899-3 (cloth : alk. paper)
    1. Wolves.   2. Wolves—Pictorial works.   I. Savage, Candace
Sherk. 1949–   Wolves.   II. Title.
QL737.C22S324   1996
599.74'442—dc20   96-17673
                                                       CIP

Front jacket photograph by Daniel J. Cox
Back jacket photograph by Alan & Sandy Carey
Jacket and book design by DesignGeist
Printed and bound in China through Mandarin Offset

10 9 8 7 6 5 4 3 2 1

The following publishers have given permission to use quoted material:
   From *Hunters in the Barrens: The Naskapi on the Edge of the White Man's World*. Copyright © 1973 by Georg Henriksen. Reprinted by permission of Memorial University of Newfoundland.
   From *Plenty-Coups, Chief of the Crows* by Frank B. Linderman. Copyright © 1930 by Frank B. Linderman. Copyright © renewed 1957 by Norma Linderman Waller, Verne. Reprinted by permissionn of HarperCollins Publishers.
   From *A Naturalist in Alaska* by Adolph Murie. Copyright © 1961 by Devin-Adair, Publishers, Inc., Old Greenwich, Connecticut 06870. Reprinted by permission of the publisher. All rights reserved.

For Diana

CONTENTS

ACKNOWLEDGEMENTS

Since 1988, when the first version of this book was published as *Wolves*, it has been warmly received by friends of the wolf around the world. I am therefore very pleased to have been asked to prepare a revised and updated version of the text and to assemble a new collection of photographs.

In the preparation of both books, my deepest debt has been to the thousands of researchers who painstakingly created the information that is reported in these pages. A few of them are named in the reference list that begins on page 102. Among them, I am especially grateful to Douglas Heard and Mark Williams, who not only shared their research libraries and reviewed early drafts of my manuscript but also took me flying over what seemed like most of northern Canada. They were also my guides and companions on the research trip to the wolf den that is described in chapter 1.

I have also benefited greatly from the generous input of wolf experts Lu Carbyn, Paul Paquet, Christoph Promberger and Jenny Ryon, each of whom went out of his or her way to provide up-to-date information. Various versions of the text have been reviewed by Lu Carbyn, L. David Mech, Jenny Ryon, Marilyn Sacks and Shelley Tanaka, all of whom made valuable suggestions for its improvement.

The production of this new edition has been greatly facilitated by the efforts of my niece Tamara Hartson and my daughter, Diana Savage, both of whom provided research assistance, and by my friend Rebecca Grambo, who undertook the initial selection of photographs. Taking our cue from the animals we were studying, we worked together with good humour and efficiency. I am grateful for their help, their skill and their enthusiasm.

FACING PAGE: *First spring.*
ALAN AND SANDY CAREY

PAGES X–XI: *Snowy shore.*
STEPHEN J. KRASEMANN,
VALAN PHOTOS

PAGE VIII: *In the words of Ernest Thompson Seton (1909), a wolf is "simply a big wild dog, living on flesh that he gets by open chase, recording his call on tree or corner stone, unsuspicious and friendly, wagging his tail for pleasure, or baying at the moon."*
TOM & PAT LEESON

Chapter 1 **WOLF MAGIC**

An ancient, empty landscape stretched out at our feet. To the east, a rocky slope flowed down to meet a broad plain, nubbly with bearberry and lichens, broken by dull blue lakes. It was August, and the land shimmered with heat.

There were four people in our party—three biologists and myself—all residents of Yellowknife in the Canadian Subarctic. To get here, we had flown north for an hour by bush plane, then slogged and scrambled across the tundra to reach this vantage point. Now our attention was focussed on the valley below and, in particular, on a sandy ridge halfway across the view. From earlier sightings, we knew that wolves had been denning there, on and off, for at least twenty years. And this year, they had returned.

There were thirteen of them in all, seven adults and six pups—a large pack for the Barren Lands. As day followed day, the adults came and went from the den like exhalations of mist. At times several would sprawl on the warm sand together, their ears flicking at bugs. The next time we checked, one or another of them would have vanished, only to appear again in an hour or a week. Every now and then, a fuzzy little pup tumbled out of the den, found a patch of shade and fell asleep.

The valley between us was hazed with insects, and little by little, our minds began to cloud with anxiety. When the adults returned to the puppies, why did they never bring meat? We knew that the nearest caribou herds could be a week's run to the north. The countryside around us was dry and motionless: a single bird twittered, a lone ground squirrel squeaked. What were the wolves eating? Why were they so lethargic? And why, one day, did the pups all slip inside the den and never come out again?

A few days later, we found a clue—a small blue-eyed corpse that had been neatly disembowelled by one of the adult wolves and buried in the moss beside a lakeshore. Starvation, we were reminded, has its own exacting code. Next year, surely, the caribou would come close to the den, so that the wolves could provision themselves. Next year, the surviving adults would prepare to breed again. Next year, perhaps, another group of observers would be there to cheer their success.

FACING PAGE: *Mexican gray wolf, an endangered subspecies.* TOM AND PAT LEESON

LIFE AND DEATH

Whatever else can be said of them, wolves are survivors. Even today they are out there, loping through the forests and across the barrens of the Northern Hemisphere. They hunt and play, feed and rest, bear their young and die, just as their ancestors have for millions of years. In fact, there are probably more wolves now than at any time in recent history. Their numbers are on the rise in several parts of the world, including the mountains of Italy and Poland; the woodlands of Russia and eastern Germany; the spruce forests of Minnesota, Michigan and Wisconsin; and the rugged valleys of Idaho, Montana, Alberta and southern British Columbia. In 1986, when a female wolf from Canada found a mate, crossed into Glacier National Park and raised a family of pups (the first in that region for fifty years), the animals were quickly dubbed the Magic Pack. Their quiet miracle, together with the welcome reappearance of wolves in other places, stands as a tribute not only to the animals' natural resilience but also to the dedication of their human well-wishers.

It has not always been so. Just a few decades ago, sensible people dedicated themselves to killing wolves, not to protecting them. Back then, reports of increasing wolf populations would scarcely have been the occasion for public rejoicing. Instead, the cry would have gone up for traps, poisons and guns, under the banner of "Death to Vermin." The goal of this clear-eyed crusade was the complete eradication of the species.

The gray wolf, *Canis lupus*, was once among the most widely distributed land mammals in the world, at home in forests, mountains, deserts and plains throughout the Northern Hemisphere. Today the species is extinct, or nearly so, over much of its natural range, and the current small-scale recoveries, however heartwarming, cannot change this fact. From Scandinavia to Portugal, Italy to Israel, and Iran to Nepal, the story is the same: only small, scattered clusters of wolves remain. The few hundred wolves that survive and breed in the Apennine Mountains of Italy obtain much of their sustenance by picking through garbage dumps. On the Iberian Peninsula, a remnant population of two to three thousand persists despite the near elimination of their natural food supply (the once plentiful herds of roe and red deer). Today, these wolves eat cows and sheep, together with poison and lead, all courtesy of local shepherds and cattle owners.

In all of Eurasia, secure populations are currently restricted to parts of eastern Europe, Russia and Mongolia. Nobody knows how many wolves are left. In Canada, where the species has been lost from about one-sixth of its original range, there may be fifty to sixty thousand. (Wolves are absent from the southernmost "settlement belt" and

FACING PAGE: *Although their coat colours range from glistening white to coal black, these wolves all belong to the same wide-ranging species:* Canis lupus, *the gray wolf.* SCOT STEWART

the Atlantic provinces.) There are probably another four to eight thousand in Alaska. Across the rest of North America, estimates are easier to come by because there is little to estimate. About two thousand wolves live and flourish in northern Minnesota—still the only significant population of wolves in the contiguous states. Elsewhere, numbers are precariously low: fifty to sixty each in Wisconsin and Michigan; about the same number in Montana and Idaho combined; a handful each in Washington, the Dakotas and Wyoming. Farther south, the species is virtually gone.

Wherever wolves have become extinct, the cause has been the same—human persecution, aggravated by habitat loss—and people are still the principal agents of death in most wolf populations. For whether we are aware of it or not, our world is also inhabited by another kind of wolf, one that lives only in the wilderness of the human mind. A shadowy, half-demonic beast, it peers out slyly from the dusk of semi-consciousness. For too long, this fictitious creature has succeeded in persuading us that it is the real wolf. This, by and large, is the animal we have hunted and killed.

If we hope now to live well with wolves, we must understand why, for so long, we have failed to do so or even to try. If we were mistaken in our hatred, how did this error originate? Why did our ancestors hold to these distorted views with such conviction? Before we can see wolves as they are, we must first clear our minds.

FACING PAGE: *Wolves need broad horizons. Their future is most secure where they have access to large, continuous regions of forest or tundra. Populations that occupy "islands" of wilderness (including most parks and wildlife reserves) become highly susceptible to extinction.* ALAN AND SANDY CAREY

Once considered a subspecies of the gray wolf, the red wolf of the southeastern United States is now recognized as a separate species, *Canis rufus. Declared extinct in the wild in 1980, the red wolf has been reintroduced to parts of northeastern North Carolina and eastern Tennessee.* TOM AND PAT LEESON

GRAY WOLF DISTRIBUTION

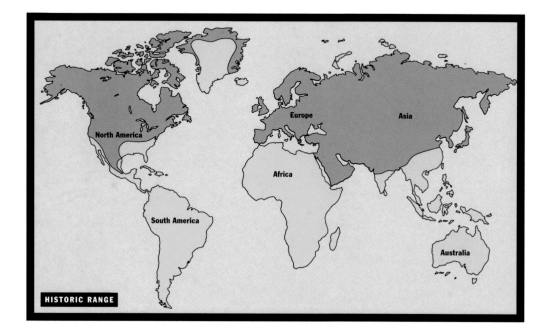

HISTORIC RANGE

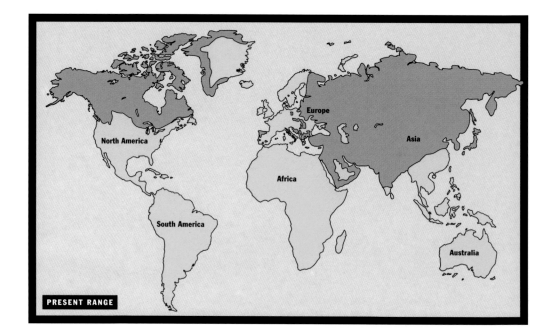

PRESENT RANGE

As the human population has expanded over the last thousand years, the wolf population has declined. By nature, wolves are at home across the northern hemisphere, from the snow fields of the high arctic, through the northern forests, and into the woodlands and grasslands of the subtropics.

ART WOLFE

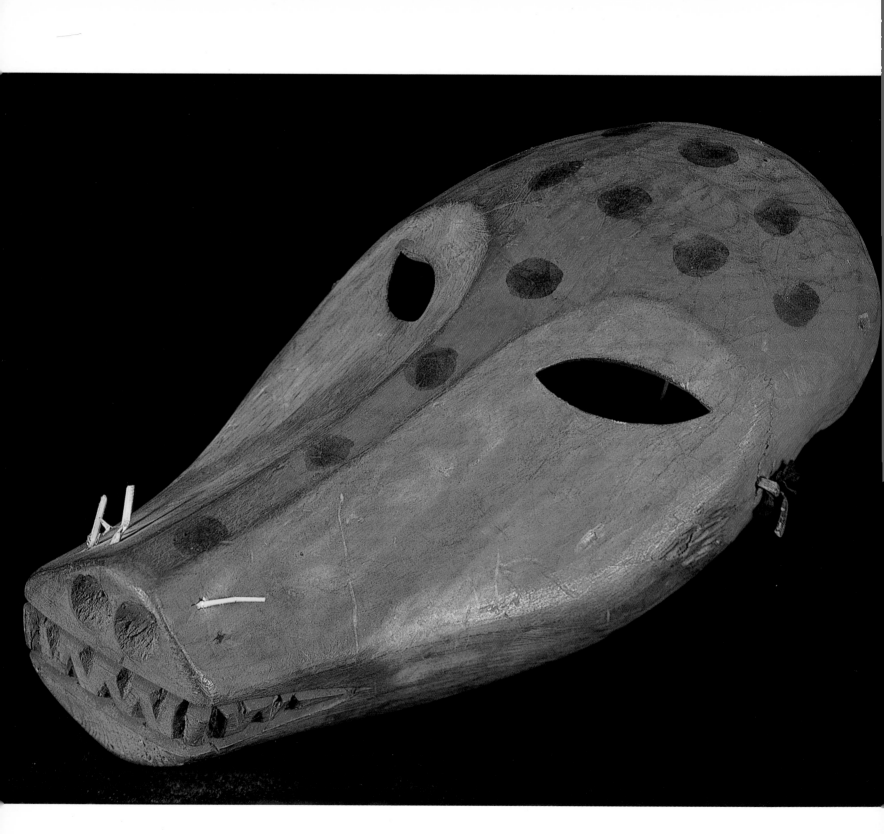

BROTHER WOLF

It is no longer possible to trace the relationship between wolves and humankind to its origins, but it probably extends back at least two million years. Even then, wolves lived much as they do today, and our far-distant ancestors may have watched them running single file through the trees, hunting hoofed animals on green prairies and bearing their pups in the comfort of sand dens. Indeed, our ancestors may have followed a similar way of life themselves, travelling in small family groupings and feasting on what they could kill. Sometimes, in ritual admiration, did these hunting people seek the wolf in themselves? Could this be why Neolithic artists sometimes sketched wolflike images on the walls of their caves?

One indirect way of exploring these ancient connections is by studying the traditions of Native Americans. Obviously, the fact that contemporary Native elders maintain certain beliefs does not tell us unequivocally what their ancestors may have thought. Nor is there any reason to suppose that all traditional peoples have cherished the same ideas through the long span of human history. Still, Native cultures offer us a glimpse into the minds of hunting people, whose vision of the world is ancestral to us all.

At the Lowrie Museum in Berkeley, California, there is a small, toothy wooden mask that was crafted more than a hundred years ago by an Eskimo carver from Alaska. In the hands of a shaman, this evocative object became the means of acquiring the abilities of a wolf, particularly its skill as a hunter. According to Arctic ethnographer Knud Rasmussen, the base of the mask was a prayer for success at killing deer, while the edge represented "the whole power of the universe—sky, earth." These powers could be approached during the full moon in December, when the shaman donned the mask. "All that we desire," the people sang, could be achieved through union with the wolf.

Half a continent to the south, the Pawnee (aboriginal people of the central United States) developed a language of hand signs. The signal for wolf was a U formed by the second and third fingers of the right hand, held beside the right ear and then brought forward. The same sign meant Pawnee.

The basis for the sympathy between human and animal hunters is not difficult to discern. In his book *Hunters in the Barrens,* anthropologist Georg Henriksen tells how the Naskapi people of Labrador search for caribou. Single file, the hunting party trots steadily away from camp, "keeping up the same speed hour after hour." They follow ridges and hilltops, scanning the landscape for prey. When they spot a herd, miles in the distance, they descend into the woods to approach it:

FACING PAGE: *According to Knud Rasmussen, Eskimo shamans used masks like this to acquire "the powers and abilities of a wolf— quickness, scent and skill at attacking animals." This elegant carving was collected at St. Michael, Alaska in the 1890s.* PHOEBE A. HEARST MUSEUM OF ANTHROPOLOGY, UNIVERSITY OF CALIFORNIA AT BERKELEY

No words are spoken. Half running, every man takes the wind, weather, and every feature of the terrain into account, and relates it to the position of the caribou. Suddenly, one of the men stops and crouches, whistling low to the other men. He has seen the herd. Without a word the men scatter in different directions. No strategy is verbalized, but each man has made up his mind about the way in which the herd can best be tackled. Seeing the other men choose their directions, he acts accordingly.

There could scarcely be a better description of the hunting behaviour of wolves.

The profound similarities between human and wolf have been celebrated in many Native American cultures for centuries. In some traditions, this kinship is believed to transcend even death, for in the spirit world, wolves are uniquely powerful. When they howl, are the spirits calling to us? According to a Cree myth, it was Wolf who, after the great flood, carried a ball of moss round and round the survivors' raft, until the Earth reformed. There is another story, too—a true one from Montana in the latter years of the nineteenth century—that tells how a Crow shaman named Bird-shirt used wolf spirit-medicine to treat a wounded warrior. His patient, Swan's-head, had been shot through the lungs in battle. Daubed with clay to resemble a wolf and carrying his ceremonial wolf skin, Bird-shirt danced. An eyewitness reported:

> Suddenly the drums changed their beating. They were softer and much faster. I heard Bird-shirt whine like a wolf-mother that has young pups, and saw him trot, as a wolf trots, around the body of Swan's-head four times. Each time he shook his rattle in his right hand, and each time dipped the nose of the wolf skin in water and sprinkled it upon Swan's-head, whining continually, as a wolf mother whines to make her pups do as she wishes.
>
> I was watching—everybody near enough was watching—when Swan's-head sat up. We then saw Bird-shirt sit down like a wolf, with his back to Swan's-head, and howl four times, just as a wolf howls four times when he is in trouble and needs help.

Bird-shirt continued to dance, to trot, to circle, to whine. He made movements with his wolf skin and, we are told, Swan's-head stood up, walked to the stream, stretched to release the black blood from his wounds and bathed in the water.

A spirit-being oversees the hunt, as a wolf follows in the footsteps of a wondrous moose. This Ojibway rock-painting graces a steep granite face on the shore of Hegman Lake in Superior National Forest, Minnesota. SCOT STEWART

MYSTERIES AND MAYHEM

Native Americans were not the only people to seek power through ritual transformation into animals. In the seventh century A.D., a council of the Christian church found it necessary to denounce people who put on the heads of beasts or "make themselves into wild animals." Some scholars contend that the European belief in werewolves (literally "man wolves") originated in just such practices. In classical Rome, for example, there were several active wolf cults. One of them centred on a god called Dis Pater, the Roman lord of death, who was often represented with a wolf's head. His priests, the "wolves of Soracte," attempted to please the gods by acting like wolves and living as predators. Another community of wolf priests was linked to the cave of Lupercal (from *lupus*, or wolf), where Romulus and Remus, the founders of Rome, had been suckled by the She-wolf. Every year, on February 15, these priests celebrated the festival of Lupercalia. Marked with the blood of a sacrificed goat, howling with ritual laughter, they paraded naked through the city, scourging any woman they met with sanctified goat hair to ensure her fertility. This outpouring of wolf magic was so important to the Roman state that the cult was reorganized and restored by Augustus.

Bizarre as this practice now seems, it is worth pausing for a moment to consider its meaning. The ritual invokes predation and death with the blood of the goat, sexuality with the nude dancing. And through those forces of blood and nakedness, the participants receive the promise of fertility, new life. This transformation is possible through the agency of the wolf, the killer, born in the cave-womb of the Earth. The festival of Lupercalia seems to have embodied the essential ambiguities of human existence—the mysteries that link birth with death, beauty with violence.

Some scholars believe that the wolf who nurtured Romulus and Remus (and thereby served as foster mother to Roman civilization) was the Etruscan goddess Lupa. In their view, the story represents both the historic antecedents of the city and the mythic antecedents of the patriarchal gods. Suggestively, the Great Goddess in her various manifestations—as Artemis, as Cerridwen—seems often to have been accompanied by wolves and dogs. Just as the deity herself was both the giver and destroyer of life, so too were her canine attendants.

Rome was not the only great culture to claim descent from the society of wolves. The Persian seer Zoroaster, the German hero Siegfried and the Turkish leader Tu Kueh are all said to have been reared by wolf mothers. Even in modern times, the concept of wolf children has retained a surprising vitality. In the 1920s, for example, an orphanage keeper in

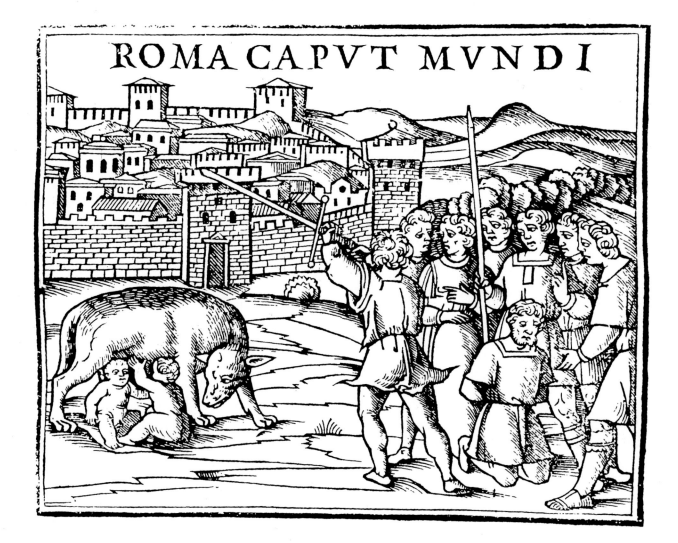

ROMA CAPVT MVNDI

This woodcut shows Romulus and Remus, the founders of Rome, in the care of a patient, bovine wolf. It originally appeared in Histoire Romaine *by Tite Live, published in 1520, and is currently held by the Musée des arts décoratifs in Paris.*

India, the Reverend Mr. Singh, claimed to have discovered two young girls in a wolf den. He found them, he said, curled up with two wolf pups and cared for by three adult wolves. The children could not walk. They preferred darkness and raw meat; they bit and howled. Had they indeed been reared by animals? Perhaps so, but two scientists who went to India in the 1950s to investigate discovered that the Reverend Mr. Singh had a disappointing reputation for untruth. A more plausible explanation has been put forward by psychologist Bruno Bettelheim, who observes that the behaviour reported for these youngsters and other so-called feral children coincides with the symptoms of severe autism. If Singh's little girls were disturbed children who had been abandoned at his orphanage, perhaps he allowed himself a small flight of fancy in accounting for their plight. After all, wolves do enjoy an intimate, playful family life, not unlike our own, so the notion that they might suckle human young is remotely plausible.

FACING PAGE: *Like indulgent human parents, wolves coddle and protect their young. Pups are given privileged access to food and can roughhouse with their elders without fear of punishment.* TOM AND PAT LEESON

RED IN TOOTH AND CLAW

If the idea of wolf children is vaguely in keeping with the facts of wolf biology, it does not accord so well with the rest of European and Euro-American wolf lore as it has come down to us. Somehow, the wolf who seemed capable of serving as a protector of infants and as an inspiration for human civilization has been supplanted by a bloodthirsty fiend. Who's afraid of the big bad wolf? Most of us are.

We have already speculated that hunting people tend to view wolves with admiration and, often, with awe. And in Europe well into classical times, wolves were associated with the most profound themes of human experience. So why have we been left with the slavering, grandmother-eating monster of Little Red Riding Hood? What motivated U.S. president Theodore Roosevelt to revile the wolf as "the beast of waste and desolation" and cry for its destruction? Why was it that one of the first acts passed by the Parliament of Upper Canada offered a cash payment to anyone who would rid the country of a wolf?

We are not talking here about carefully monitored wolf "control." We are talking about a hysterical hatred that eventually led to the near extermination of wolves from western Europe, the contiguous United States and southern Canada.

This passion—which has by no means been entirely extinguished—was fuelled by the fear of economic loss. Wolves specialize in killing large, hoofed mammals: moose, deer, muskoxen, caribou and, sometimes, sheep, goats and cows. Wolf predation on livestock has troubled herders and ranchers (including frontier cattlemen like Teddy Roosevelt) since the earliest days of agriculture. According to a Greek text from the second century A.D., the technique for killing wolves with poisoned meat can be traced back through antiquity to the god Apollo. From the moment that humans began to tend flocks, wolves were forced into the role of villain.

Fear breeds fear; hatred breeds hatred. Enveloped in a dark cloud of anxious imaginings, wolves attained a fearful reputation for gluttony. On the one hand, they were accused of unbridled depredations on livestock, though in fact they almost always prefer wild prey. On the other, they were denounced for craving human flesh, though in fact they do not generally hunt down human beings. To be sure, wolves do occasionally attack people, but such events have been extraordinarily rare, at least in our era. Indeed, wolf experts L. David Mech and the late Douglas Pimlott assert that a healthy North American wolf never poses a significant threat to human beings. Notice the caveats: they say "healthy" because rabid wolves are unequivocally dangerous; and "North American" because European wolves may be somewhat more aggressive than those in the New

World. According to Finnish biologist Erkki Pullianen, several people have been killed by wolves in Finland and Russia in recent decades. But, astonishingly, the number of documented fatalities in North America stands at zero. The few confrontations that have occurred have generally ended less happily for the wolves than for their human "victims."

In ten years of radio-collaring wolves and caribou, wildlife biologists in the Northwest Territories have been attacked only twice. One of the wolves was rabid; the second was interested in a caribou that the biologists were working on. In both cases, the people escaped with nothing worse than nightmares.

Across northern Canada, every community has an attendant population of wolves that live on the outskirts and survive as scavengers. The animals are extremely wary and seldom show themselves, though every now and then local schoolchildren are warned to take care because a wolf has been seen in town. Even in the North, few adults realize that the animals are always around and that the only fatalities on record have been dogs.

And then there are the thousands of people who canoe and camp in the wolf country of Ontario's Algonquin Park every summer. Yet we never hear of injuries, or even of close calls, for the simple reason that they don't happen.

One final example is worth mention because it is so astonishing. In the mid-1950s, a researcher named D. F. Parmelee and a companion captured two wolf pups on Ellesmere Island in the Canadian Arctic. They then shot several ptarmigan and headed back to camp, the pups in their arms, the birds dangling over their shoulders. Suddenly they sensed something behind them. They turned around to discover the bereaved female wolf, "her nose touching the ptarmigans as they swayed back and forth." Parmelee writes, "Incredible as it surely is, we several times had to drive that wolf off with snowballs for fear that we would lose our specimens!" The wolf spent the night outside the researchers' tent, harming neither the humans nor their acquisitions.

This is the true nature of wolves. Their normal response to people is not aggression but curiosity or fear. What then do we make of the notorious "beasts of Gévaudan," two animals that, in the 1760s, are reported to have killed up to a hundred people, mostly small children, in south-central France? How do we account for claims in a century-old scientific monograph that 161 people in Russia were killed and eaten in 1875, or reputable reports that two villagers in northwest Turkey met a similar fate during a blizzard in 1968? Some of these stories do have a partial basis in fact: careful research has determined that the killers at Gévaudan were probably a small number of wolf-dog hybrids, which combined the wolf's strength and savvy with the dog's orientation towards people. Once people decided these "wolves" were monstrous, they launched an assault on the entire species. Over a period of about thirty years, two thousand wolves were killed in misplaced retribution.

Figure du Monstre, qui desole le Gévaudan,
Cette Bête est de la taille d'un jeune Taureau elle attaque de préférence les Femmes,
et les Enfans elle boit leur Sang, leur coupe la Tête et l'emporte.
Il est promis 2700 tt à qui tuerait cet animal

This eighteenth-century engraving, from the Bibliothèque nationale of France, shows the monster that desolated the region of Gévaudan in the years following 1764. According to the caption, the beast was the size of a young bull and had a preference for killing women and children.

A lone wolf croons to the setting sun.
Although wolves don't howl at the
moon as legend suggests, they are
most likely to raise their voices in
the torchlight of dusk or dawn.
ALAN AND SANDY CAREY

WOLVES IN THE GARDEN

Our false beliefs about wolves are responsible for most reports of wolf attacks. Such stories have less to do with the biology of wild animals than with the psychology of western European Christianity over several tormented centuries. Wolves speak to the human mind with the power of myth: they represent the energy of the Earth, the passions of human life and death. These include sex. It is not by accident that the Latin words for "wolf" and "whore" are identical, that in English we refer to a sexually aggressive man as a wolf, and that when a girl has her first intercourse, French speakers say "*elle a vu le loup.*" For many centuries, Christianity was at war with human sexuality; the World, the Flesh and the Devil were potent and menacing.

Therefore it is not surprising to learn that by the time of the Inquisition, the wolf had been equated with Satan—the "wolf" in Christ's fold. In the words of Barry Lopez, in his classic study *Of Wolves and Men*, "there was a great mystery about the wolf and a fabulous theater of images developed around him. He was the Devil, red tongued, sulphur breathed, and yellow eyed; he was the werewolf, human cannibal; he was the lust, greed, and violence that men saw in themselves." All that we most feared and hated in ourselves, we projected onto our age-old companions, the animals with which we felt the greatest kinship. And so wolves were to be killed, brutally if possible, to rid the world of sin. Werewolves, too, were tortured until they confessed to shape shifting and gory sexual crimes, and then were executed.

When Europeans arrived en masse in North America, they brought with them eighteenth-century versions of these same lurid misconceptions. To them was added a new concomitant: a struggle against the wilderness that was both literal and mythic. The settlers arrived with a mission to tend a garden in a wild land. There was no place in the garden for predators. Wolves were killers and, in addition to any actual threat, reminded the newcomers that they were ultimately not in control, even in this new and promised land.

On both continents wolves were persecuted with fury: hundreds of thousands were slaughtered. In North America they were trapped and poisoned by ranchers, bounty hunters and professional "wolfers." In the melodramatic spirit of the American West, the last survivors in each area were described as outlaws and given bandit names: "Three Toes," "Mountain Billy" and "Custer Wolf." A hundred and fifty men tried to kill Three Toes and collect the gold watch offered in reward. It was all very exciting. Between 1883 and 1918, bureaucrats in Montana alone paid out on 80,730 claims for wolf bounty.

FACING PAGE: *"Everybody believes to some degree that wolves howl at the moon, or weigh two hundred pounds, or travel in packs of fifty, or are driven crazy by the smell of blood,"* Barry Lopez points out. *"None of this is true."* The truth is that we know little about the wolf as it is and a great deal more about the wolf as we imagine it. THOMAS KITCHIN, FIRST LIGHT

We cannot distance ourselves from this carnage by declaring that the people who accomplished it were evil. Many of the wolf killers were civil servants hired by democratically elected governments to carry out the public will. Virtually everyone was of the same mind: the country should be cleared of wolves. In 1907, the U. S. Department of Agriculture released a *Guide to Finding and Killing Wolves*, "to be issued to as many ranchers, hunters, trappers and forest rangers as possible." In 1909, the superintendent of Algonquin Park wrote an article entitled "How should we destroy the wolf?" Not "Should we?"—that could be taken for granted even by an official custodian of nature—just "How?" In the early sixties, when the first careful study of wolves in the park was undertaken, it ended with a determined effort to "collect" the carcasses of wolves from the study area.

That was only thirty years ago, yet today such an action would be unthinkable. Although a few people are still fogged in by the prejudices of bygone times, a fresh wind has blown through the public mind. Perhaps the enthusiasm of the sixties succeeded in lightening our spirits. Certainly Hiroshima, *Silent Spring* and the subtle new science of ecology have gradually changed our thinking. Wolves, which just a short time ago were burdened with all that was bestial and menacing in nature and in ourselves, suddenly have become the symbols of a born-again wilderness.

"In wildness," Thoreau told us, "is the preservation of the world." Many of us, with the fervour that comes of knowing life itself may be at risk, have placed our hopes on the side of the wolves and wilderness.

People deeply at odds with themselves have been at odds with wolves. So it is a sign of great hope that we find ourselves drawn to them with renewed sympathy. Yet our change of heart will be of little significance if we merely become engrossed in a new mythic drama, with wolves now cast as shining heroes and their human critics assigned to play the black-hearted villains. We cannot spend our lives on the set of a Walt Disney film, where wolves are nice puppies that eat only mice, and every person who kills an animal is a shady character. Reality, as we currently understand it, is more interesting—and more challenging—than that.

FACING PAGE: *Before Europeans arrived in North America, "the whole continent was one continual dismal wilderness, the haunt of wolves." At least that was the melancholy vision of John Adams, who served as U.S. president at the end of the eighteenth century.*
DENVER BRYAN

FACING PAGE: *According to a First Nations myth, the spirits once tried to transform all the animals into humans but only succeeded in changing the eyes of the wolf.*
TOM AND PAT LEESON

Chapter 2 **WILD LIVES**

The itch of human curiosity being what it is, there are probably many things you want to know about wolves: how big they get, how fast they run, how many pups they have, whether it's really true that they can communicate over long distances. You may be interested in their family lives, their hunting strategies and their importance as predators.

Surprisingly, the best place to begin this exploration is inside a wolf's mouth. Wolves have forty-two teeth, which fall into the same general categories as our own—incisors, canines, premolars and molars. Three special features of this arsenal call for our attention: first, the sheer number of teeth. (Mountain lions, by contrast, have only thirty.) The need to make room for them all and deploy them usefully probably accounts for the wolf's long snout. Notice next the four pointed canines, or "dog teeth," near the front of the jaw on the bottom and top. As long as penknife blades, these teeth are the functional equivalent of talons and permit a wolf to pierce through tough hides and thick hair—and hang on. Thus equipped, a wolf can bite through the flesh of a woolly muskox or hook its fangs into the pendulous nose of a moose and cling fast, no matter how much the animal thrashes about.

The third feature to note is the set of massive craggy molars towards the back of the mouth. (They can be glimpsed in the photograph on page 68.) These specialized shearing teeth, known as carnassials, are one of the reasons that the modern line of carnivores has managed to survive. You could find them, if you dared, in the mouths of bears, weasels, tigers and the two hundred other members of the order Carnivora, the evolutionary line to which wolves belong.

You could also find them, at less personal risk, in the mouth of a pet dog. In fact, you would find all forty-two wolf teeth there, in somewhat modified form. This is because wolves and dogs are close kin. Although the subject continues to be controversial, most authorities agree that all dogs, from chihuahuas to Dobermanns, are descended from wolves that were tamed in the Near East ten thousand to twelve thousand years ago.

FACING PAGE: *A snarling wolf displays a sample of its forty-two specialized teeth, including several sharp incisors and a dagger-like "dog tooth."* DANIEL J. COX

Others speculate that wolves were domesticated then and at several other places and times. There is no longer any serious argument in favour of another species as a major point of origin—coyote, fox or any other member of the wild dog family. (In North America, coyotes, wolves and dogs all occasionally interbreed to produce coy-wolf, coy-dog and wolf-dog hybrids, so it is likely that the dog line carries a little coyote blood.)

Why were wolves singled out for this intimate recognition as the first domesticated animal and "man's best friend"? To answer this question, we must look at the ways in which wolves differ from other members of the wild dog family. For one thing, wolves take first place for size. Although smaller in fact than in legend, adult females weigh between about 20 and 55 kilograms (45 and 120 pounds), and males may be 70 kilograms (155 pounds) or more. On average, tip to tail, they measure about 1.5 metres (4 to 5 feet) in length and stand .75 metres (2½ feet) high at the shoulder. They are, in other words, very big dogs, larger in every dimension than a standard German shepherd. By taming wolves, people allied themselves with this impressive strength and size.

Early hunting people also took advantage of wolves' superior speed. More than any other carnivores, these far-ranging animals are adapted to run. For one thing, they and other wild dogs enjoy a runner's leggy build. For another, canines have moved up off the flat of their feet and onto their toes for extra speed. But the specialization that sets wolves apart is the anatomy of their front legs, which are "hung" close together, almost as if pressed into the animals' narrow chests. Their knees turn in and their paws turn outward, allowing their front feet to set a path which the hind feet follow precisely. When they are trotting, wolves leave a neat, single line of tracks, an advantage for efficient travel in deep snow or on difficult terrain. Thanks to these physical refinements, wolves can run at 60 to 70 kilometres (35 to 45 miles) per hour when pressed.

FACING PAGE: *Most breeds of dogs have shorter snouts than wolves do. This is the result of a human preference for pets that look a little more like us and a little less like their "nosy" wild cousins.*
NORBERT ROSING

Travelling at a steady, swinging trot, wolves can easily travel 50 kilometres (30 miles) a day, even in the depths of winter. When they put on a burst of speed, they can literally make the snow fly.
THOMAS KITCHIN, FIRST LIGHT

FAMILY VALUES

The aspect of the wolf's nature that may have had the strongest appeal to the first would-be dog owners, as it does for us today, is the animals' affectionate interest in their families. More than any other canid, wolves are social animals. Although some individuals live singly for periods of time (the proverbial "lone wolves"), the usual context of a wolf's life is a small kinship grouping, or pack, that includes mother and father, uncles and aunts, and siblings. Pack sizes, like most other wolf traits, vary considerably, from a single pair, which is quite common, to a community of forty-two (recorded in northern Alberta), which is very rare. Most wolves live in groups of seven animals or less.

The overriding theme of wolf society is amiability. In the early 1940s, a patient biologist named Adolph Murie spent two summers observing at a wolf den in Denali (then Mount McKinley) National Park in Alaska, as part of the first-ever scientific study of wild wolves. "The strongest impression remaining with me after watching the wolves on numerous occasions," he wrote, "was their friendliness." This was despite all the inevitable irritations of family life: a pup who wants to jump on your head, a sibling who hogs the best sleeping place, an elder who eats more than his share, and so on.

One key to the generally even-tempered atmosphere of a wolf pack is clear communication. Like people, wolves have expressive faces. Through subtle gestures of the forehead, mouth, ears and eyes, an animal can "say" how it feels and thus permit its companions to react appropriately. For example, if a wolf is afraid or insecure, it keeps its teeth covered ("see, I would never bite you"), pulls the corners of its mouth back in a smilelike "submissive grin," narrows its eyes to slanting slits, smooths its forehead and flattens its ears against its head. A confident, threatening expression is just the reverse: bared teeth, mouth corners forward, wrinkled muzzle, frowning forehead and erect, forward-pointing ears. Human expressions are amazingly similar. Try making an ingratiating face, as if you want to ease out of a confrontation with a bully; then scowl as if you are ready to bite off someone's head. Chances are you won't be able to say much with your ears, but otherwise your facial gestures will likely resemble those of a wolf in similar circumstances.

It is much easier for a human being to intuit the mood of a wolf or dog than that of a hamster, say, or a canary. As photographer Jim Brandenburg put it after a summer spent watching wolves in the high Arctic, "I've never seen animals that have so many characteristics that can be felt." No wonder early people chose wolves for their companions.

If the first dog was pure wolf, modern dogs are so distinct from their ancestors that they are considered by many scientists to be a separate species. *Canis lupus* has become

FACING PAGE: *With their alert ears, rounded eyes and relaxed mouths, these wolves are the very picture of contentment. The black-and-white markings on the ears, eyes and lips draw attention to the animals' most expressive features.* ALAN AND SANDY CAREY

OVERLEAF: *A wolf that has been dining alone (right) is forced to share its meal with a group of disgruntled pack members. Although the newcomers are lunging onto the scene with apparent confidence, their laid-back ears reveal a measure of anxiety or fear.* ART WOLFE

Canis familiaris. In addition to the obvious differences that have been bred into certain lines, other more subtle changes have taken place. Even the most wolflike of modern dogs tend to have smaller teeth, shorter muzzles and broader foreheads than wolves, making them look a little more like their human masters. They are also said to be less intelligent than their wild cousins, a common result of domestication. (It would be interesting to know if this rule holds for humans, as well.) Dogs breed twice a year rather than once, lack certain glands on the tail and have distinctively shaped skulls. To human eyes, their feet seem to be "the right size," rather than "too big" like those of their snowshoed, wild relatives. But the most significant difference is in their social attitude: dogs want to be with people, wolves want to be with wolves. The bonds of affection that connect a dog to its favourite humans are probably very similar to those that form among a pack of wolves.

FACING PAGE: *Its tail wagging with pleasure, a wolf lands one of its snowshoe paws on the back of a playmate.* ALAN AND SANDY CAREY

PEACE, ORDER AND GOOD GOVERNMENT

Wolf packs are loosely hierarchical. A large, well-established pack may consist of a small "upper class" that includes only a single breeding pair (the so-called alpha male and female), a "middle class" of nonbreeding adults, perhaps an "underclass" of outcasts, and an up-and-coming group of pups and immature animals who are less than two years of age. The leaders of the pack, usually the parents of the younger animals, wear their status with confidence. In social encounters, they stand tall, hold their ears and tails erect, and look other animals directly in the eyes. Simply by doing this, they are declaring and reinforcing their superior rank. A subordinate animal, on the other hand, slips towards the leader on bent legs, tail low and ears slicked back. Like a pup begging for food, it bunts its nose against the superior's face in greeting, as if to say, "I'm little and you're big; I like you, so please be nice to me." This gesture has been dubbed "active submission." If the subordinate animal feels a need to make its point more emphatically—"I accept that you are the leader and that I am a social underling; I'm no threat to you"—it may sprawl on its back with its feet in the air, exactly like a dog that wants its belly scratched. This behaviour, known as "passive submission," may also carry a reference to infancy, because it is very like the position of a tiny pup that is being massaged by an adult to make its bowels work. You can look for these dominance/submission routines in the wolf cage at the zoo, or see how the wolves react if you use your hands to mimic ears-up and ears-back postures. (Ironically, most of our intimate knowledge of these spirits of the wilderness has been gained by observing animals in captivity.)

With a bit of luck, you may also have a chance to watch a wolf greeting ceremony, one of those noisy, wagful, face-licking get-togethers in which the animals rediscover one another after waking from a snooze or reunite after a brief separation. In the wild, these celebrations of family solidarity also often occur when the animals first scent prey before a hunt or after a kill. Frequently, the focus of the festivities is the alpha male—often the most popular animal in the pack—who suddenly finds himself closely surrounded by half a dozen eager, howling relatives, all doing their best to plaster up beside him and stick their muzzles in his face. Through this affectionate ritual, the animals define their group ("this is us; all other wolves are outsiders") and reaffirm their attachment to their father and to one another.

As a rule, a dominant male wolf is not particularly aggressive, at least towards other members of his group. In fact, the opposite is likely to be true: most top-ranking male wolves are exceptionally tolerant. Wolves in a pack are constantly checking one another,

FACING PAGE: By lowering its ears and drooping its eyelids, the wolf on the left submits to a determined companion. Although high-ranking (alpha) animals could win all disputes if they chose to do so, they often prefer to give way in minor contests over food and other resources. PETER MCLEOD, FIRST LIGHT

with a sniff to the coat here, a lick on the cheek there; and no animal is more active in receiving this kind of routine social contact than the dominant male. He provides an emotional centre for the community and a focus for friendly feeling in the pack. One of his most important social functions is to help maintain the even temper and cohesiveness of the family. If he loses his position to a younger male in a coup (as happens from time to time), he will probably also lose his ability to serve the pack in this way.

FACING PAGE: *A group of wolves romp together in a display of mutual affection and attachment. By placing its nose under its companion's muzzle, the animal in the centre makes a friendly gesture of subordinance.* VICTORIA HURST, FIRST LIGHT

HOMELANDS

Another important responsibility of top-ranking animals (both males and females) is maintaining the pack's hunting territory. As a Russian proverb observes, "The wolf is kept fed by his feet." But this does not mean that the animals travel aimlessly across the countryside. Instead, most packs restrict their journeys to the familiar trails and terrain of a large tract of land. Just how large depends on the size of the pack and the density of prey that is available. On northeastern Vancouver Island, British Columbia, for example, where black-tailed deer are abundant, a pack of ten wolves was found to occupy an area of only about 60 square kilometres (25 square miles). In Michigan, by contrast, where food is less plentiful, a group of four required 650 square kilometres (250 square miles), and in Alberta, a pack of eight ranged over more than 1300 square kilometres (500 square miles). Just as a statistically average person, with its 1.3 mates and 1.6 offspring, is an improbable fiction, so is a numerically average wolf territory. A territory might be as small as 50 or as large as 1500 square kilometres (20 to 600 square miles)—a thirtyfold variability. What's more, territorial boundaries are dynamic, as the animals expand and contract their range in response to changes in their food supply. This extraordinary capacity to adapt to current conditions is one of the reasons that wolves were formerly so widespread and are now so resilient.

Whatever the size of the territory, that area is the pack's home ground and more-or-less exclusive domain. The resident animals are sometimes tolerant of outsiders and allow them to cross their land (and even to hunt) without harassment. But often intruders will receive a rough reception. Adolph Murie tells of a spring morning in Alaska when he watched a pack of wolves laze around their den. As the younger animals dozed in the pale sunshine, the leading male fidgeted uneasily and then moved to a lookout just above the others. What was upsetting him? "Shortly after noon the four wolves at the den joined [him] and they all bunched up, wagging tails and expressing much friendliness." That was when Murie noticed a sixth wolf,

a small gray animal, about 50 yards from the others. All the [resident] wolves trotted to the stranger and practically surrounded it, and for a few moments I thought that they would be friendly toward it for there was just the suggestion of tail wagging by some of them. But something tipped the scales the other way for the wolves began to bite at the stranger. It rolled over on its back, begging quarter. The attack continued, however, so it scrambled to its feet and with difficulty emerged from the snapping wolves. Twice it was knocked over as it ran down the slope with the five wolves in hot pursuit.

FACING PAGE: *Although wolves are capable of killing each other, it is extremely rare for them to do so. Most disagreements are settled without bloodshed and are over and forgotten in a few minutes.* TOM WALKER

Four of the wolves soon abandoned the chase, but the leading male drove on, giving the intruder no option but flight. Says Murie, "The unfortunate stranger's hip and base of tail were soaked with blood. It was completely discouraged in its attempt to join the group, for it was not seen again." Had it persisted, it might have been killed.

For the most part, wolves avoid this kind of bloodshed by keeping out of foreign territories. Each pack's holdings are thoroughly posted with No Trespassing signs in the form of "scent posts." These are simply conspicuous objects—stumps, logs, rocks, chunks of ice, and so on—along trails, at crossroads and, especially, near the edges of the territory, which the wolves mark by urinating on them. This medium of communication may not be very elegant by human standards, but it works. Most of the marking is done by the dominant male and female, who dole out their urine in dribbles every few hundred metres. (This explains why it can take so long to walk the dog!) Sometimes a whole line of wolves will wait patiently for a turn to leave their mark on a scent post. Perhaps this is another way of demonstrating group solidarity for, as researcher Russ Rothman once observed, "Wolves that pee together stay together."

COMMON SCENTS

Wolves have an extraordinary sense of smell—in the right wind, they can detect a moose at more than 2 kilometres (1½ miles)—and they probably obtain a great deal of information from their scent marks. They may even use them to find their way around. Through experience, wolves are believed to develop mental maps of their territories, on which locations such as kill sites and trail junctions are registered. Thus it is probably significant that the crossroads of trails—the decision points for efficient route-finding—are generously scent-marked, making them vivid and memorable.

Because our own sense of smell is weak, we are at a loss to properly decode these olfactory messages, but it seems possible that wolves pick up more personal details as well: which individuals, of which sex, were last here; who is travelling with whom; and how long it has been since the area was hunted. At the very least, it is clear that they can distinguish between fresh marks and old ones, and can tell when they pick up a stranger's scent. Wolves seem to scent-mark more frequently near the edges than in the centre of their territories, perhaps because they can detect the scent of their neighbours in the borderlands. (There is often a narrow band of overlap, about a kilometre wide, which adjacent packs explore at different times.) The foreign odours apparently stimulate the animals to leave their mark on the disputed zone and then to turn around and head for the safety of their own ground.

Assuming that they are relatively well fed, wolves sometimes choose to give up a meal rather than risk trespassing on another pack's land. Biologists working in northeastern Minnesota tell the story of a pack that had chased and wounded a deer. The prey was badly hurt, yet on it ran, with the wolves on its heels. But when it crossed a river that served as the dividing line between two territories, the wolves followed for a short distance, then stopped, scent-marked and trotted back home. The next day, the neighbouring pack killed and ate the deer.

WOLF TALK

Another way wolves lay claim to their territories is with sound. Wolves are chatty creatures. In close-up communication, they use a variety of noises—whimpers, whines, squeaks, yelps, barks, snarls and growls—to express their emotions. For long-distance communication, they raise their voices in that most evocative of all wolf sounds, their cool, lingering howl. The powerful effect of this song on human listeners is mystifying. Why should these rising harmonies, uttered by another species for communication with its own kind, resonate so strongly in the human psyche? In recent years, thousands of people have had a chance to experience this reaction at first hand by participating in wolf howls. Picture a long line of cars creeping through the dusk of a wilderness park, then rolling to a stop. The occupants quickly step out, turn their faces to the sky—howl—then listen. About one time in ten, the human howlers are rewarded by a response, for just as people respond psychically to wolves, so wolves often answer people directly. This fact has been used by wildlife biologists to get an idea of wolf densities in certain areas. The more frequently the biologists get a response, the greater the number of wolves are presumed to be present.

Curiously, this technique does not work nearly so well if the human howls are recorded instead of live. Wolves are much less likely to answer recordings. Although human ears cannot distinguish between the two sources, tests reveal very slight distortions on the tapes. If the wolves can detect these minor anomalies, imagine what they might be able to discern in natural howls.

Just as each person has a unique singing voice, so individual wolves have distinct howls. For example, a particular wolf may always begin and end in a certain way, stay within a certain range of pitches, or include a specific jump from pitch to pitch. Can wolves recognize one another at a distance by these characteristics? Does a howl reveal what the animal is doing or how it is feeling? It has been proven that a wolf that is walking slowly howls slightly differently than if it were lying down or pacing, and one that is sending out an unsolicited message sings higher than if it were responding to another animal. Some people think the howling of a wolf that is isolated from its companions broadcasts a particularly plaintive, lonesome-sounding call. Whether or not wolves can send messages such as "the hunting over here is pretty bad and I am going to stay another week," as Farley Mowat would have us believe, definitely remains to be seen.

As nearly as we can tell, wolves often howl simply because they love to. A group howl (the "greeting ceremony" described earlier) has been likened to a community singsong.

FACING PAGE: Like blues singers pouring out their souls, wolves throw their heads back and close their eyes when they howl. ERWIN AND PEGGY BAUER

According to Lois Crisler, who kept free-ranging wolves in Alaska for several years, some animals "will run from any distance, panting and bright-eyed, to join in, uttering, as they near, fervent little wows, jaws wide, hardly able to wait to sing." Each animal joins in at its own pitch for, as Crisler observed, "wolves avoid unison singing; they like chords." A typical howling bout lasts just over a minute, with a pause of at least twenty minutes between sessions. By participating in these festivities, wolves probably strengthen the amicable feeling between themselves and other members of the pack.

Howling also serves to reunite the pack physically if members have separated to hunt alone or in small groups. Wolves have an uncanny ability to pinpoint the source of a howl and use it to locate their companions. In open terrain, a mere human can hear howls 15 kilometres (10 miles) away and, if the sounds are muffled by woods, at half that distance. A wolf's hearing is, of course, more far-reaching than our own.

In addition to providing long-distance communication among pack members, howls also serve as a means of contact between packs. On a calm night, a single howling bout can advertise a pack's presence over an area of more than 130 square kilometres (50 square miles). Researchers think that howling is a means of territorial defence among wolves, just as singing is among many species of birds. "This land is our land," the wolf pack cries; and the neighbouring pack may reply, "And this is ours." Sometimes as many as three packs will chorus back and forth, each within its own territory; then each will retreat from its neighbours.

Although wolves may howl alone and at any time of the year, they do most of their singing in groups, during the winter. This pack is assembling for a "greeting ceremony," a jubilant celebration of family togetherness. PETER MCLEOD, FIRST LIGHT

SEXUAL POLITICS

By now you may have concluded that the defence of territories (laying claim to familiar den sites, resting places, travel routes and food resources) is a basic characteristic of wolves. And so it is—with several notable exceptions. Packs that normally maintain separate territories may occasionally cluster together around rich sources of food, such as deer yards or bison herds. And some wolves do not seem to be territorial at any time. Tundra wolves, for example, do not hold territories because they cannot afford to stay in one area. Their primary prey, the Barren Ground caribou, undergoes a dramatic annual cycle of migrations, sweeping south to the forests for winter, north to the tundra to calve, taking a certain route one year, dodging hundreds of kilometres to the east or west the next, defying all prediction by either human or wolf. Except for spring and early summer when they are denning, tundra wolves are also migratory, trailing the herds up and down the northern third of the continent. What role scent-marking and howling might play for these animals, or even how they organize and maintain their packs, is not yet understood.

One hint that a different social system may operate among tundra wolves than elsewhere is the high percentage of northern females that become pregnant every year. This is not at all the case in territorial packs where, typically, only one female and one male—usually the highest-ranking animals—breed in a given season. Sometimes this happens because the alpha pair are the only sexually mature animals in the pack, the others being youngsters less than two years of age. But even in packs that include several adults of each sex, the general rule is that only the "top dogs" will bear young. Research suggests that 94 per cent of wild wolf packs produce only one litter per year, and that nearly 40 per cent of mature females fail to reproduce each season.

This birth control is achieved through social interaction. Strictly speaking, the breeding season lasts for about four weeks in late winter, sometime between January and April, depending on latitude. It is during this period that the adult females come into oestrus, or heat, and are able to reproduce. But preparations for mating begin much earlier, often in the fall, and are marked by a sudden increase in social tension: snarling, snapping, fighting. Although the males do most of the scrapping, the dominant female is the one who makes the most dangerous attacks. Her animosity is directed mainly towards the other adult females, some of whom fail to become fertile as a result of the stress she inflicts upon them. Under constant assault, these animals often become temporary outcasts, forced to live on the fringes of group activity.

When the actual mating time comes, it is the leading female and not one of her

FACING PAGE: *The alpha female decides whom she will accept as a mate and when she will do so. Here, she temporarily spurns the attentions of her partner, a large white male.*
DANIEL J. COX

oppressed subordinates who initiates courtship. She does this by making gestures of sexual interest in the presence of high-ranking males and by squirting urine on bushes, trees, rocks and other places where it is likely to be noticed. At first the males do not seem to know what is going on, but after a while they catch the excitement of the season and start crowding around her, touching her muzzle, snuffling her body, sniffing her ambrosial pee, peeing on her ambrosial pee—ah, bliss. Soon all the males in the pack, even the pups, may be following in her wake.

They will not, however, all have a chance to breed. In large part, the choice is made by the female, who likes some of the males and rejects others. But the top-ranking male also gets into the act by attempting to prevent other males from mating. So we now have a situation in which the alpha female is continuing to suppress her same-sex rivals, and the alpha male has begun to do the same. The only opportunities that subordinate animals have to mate occur when the dominant pair is busy. One young male got his chance when the alpha male was feeding; a second pair was able to breed when the dominant animals were literally "tied up." (Like dogs, mating wolves remain physically attached in a copulatory tie for about half an hour.)

FACING PAGE: *Although the male mounts the female by standing over her back, he swings round as soon as their genitals become attached. The animals lie quietly, tail to tail, until the copulatory "tie" is relaxed.*
DANIEL J. COX

The even temper of the pack is disrupted during the mating season, when the top-ranking female begins to oppress the other females in the group. Some animals are so traumatized by this persecution that they fail to come into breeding condition. TOM AND PAT LEESON

THE COURSE OF TRUE LOVE

It has often been said that wolves mate for life, and it does seem to be true that breeding animals tend to choose the same partners in successive years. But this is not the result of a hearts-and-flowers till-death-do-us-part loyalty. To be sure, wolves do form strong bonds with one another, but these preferences are not exclusive. Besides, they can only be expressed sexually if the social order permits. In one captive pack, for example, the alpha female wanted to mate with the alpha male, but he preferred the third-ranked bitch. The female then accepted the second-ranked, or beta, male, though the alpha male tried to stop this mating. Both alpha animals snarled and bit at the beta male while he was copulating with the alpha female. The next year, the alpha male was absent, so the female again accepted the beta male, along with two others. The males were interested in other females, and other females wanted to breed, but the alpha female prevented these matings by interfering.

The alpha female died the next year as the result of leg wounds inflicted by the most suppressed female. Had she survived this injury, she might well have become a pack outcast, a common fate for deposed alphas. She would then have left the group or become its most submissive, hangdog member, while her successor acquired the social power and sexual privilege of high office. Had she dropped out of the pack in the wild, she might have wandered widely until she met a lone male and joined with him to initiate a new family.

If the social structure is disrupted by the death of key individuals, the pack's social system breaks down, and contraception cannot always be imposed. Where wolves are hunted or otherwise persecuted by people, for example, a high percentage of females is likely to breed. Even in the far north of Canada, where the small human population raises the possibility that wolves might live in relative peace, biologists are beginning to suspect that it is human hunting and not a unique social pattern that leads to the animals' unusual fecundity.

FACING PAGE: *Like a kiss on the cheek, a "muzzle bite" is an expression of gentle, affectionate feelings towards the recipient.* ALAN AND SANDY CAREY

NURSERY TALES

When the females' period of oestrus ends, the agitated atmosphere of the breeding season gradually fades. If subordinate females have been suppressed, they are now readmitted to the fellowship of the pack and may even help the alpha female prepare her den. This may involve simply cleaning out a burrow that has been used in previous years, since some dens are occupied for decades; or it may mean enlarging and renovating an old fox burrow or an abandoned beaver lodge. Alternatively, the female may decide to excavate a new hole, generally choosing a sandy hillside that promises easy digging through the still-frozen ground. She also gives preference to sites that are near a supply of drinking water from a spring, river or lake. Work on the den or dens (the female may prepare several) often begins about six weeks after she conceives and three weeks before the pups are born. The gestation period for wolves is about sixty-three days.

What is it like inside a wolf den? Adolph Murie decided to find out. "I wriggled into the burrow which was 16 inches high and 25 inches wide. Six feet from the entrance of the burrow there was a right angle turn. At the turn there was a hollow, rounded and worn, which obviously was a bed much used by an adult . . . From the turn the burrow slanted slightly upward for 6 feet" to a chamber for the pups.

It is to these snug surroundings that the female retires alone to give birth. As each tiny infant appears, the mother licks it hard to remove the amniotic sac, chews through the umbilical cord, then licks the baby again until it is clean, dry and snuggled against her side. It takes her about three hours to whelp a typical litter of five or six pups. At birth, the pups can do little but squirm and suck; their awareness scarcely extends beyond warmth and warm milk. But after a couple of weeks, their eyes begin to focus, dimly at first, and by three weeks they can walk, chew, growl and hear. It is at about this time that they first poke their round heads out of the den; then let the fun begin!

Everyone who has played with a puppy dog knows how delightfully silly and full of life they are. A wolf pup is just the same, and five or six of them, growing up together in the fresh spring air, form an exuberant company. "Catch me if you can." "Don't look now! I'm going to pounce on you." "Watch me kill this old piece of caribou hide!" "I can beat up on you." All these puppy games have their serious side, since the youngsters are practising hunting skills, learning the subtleties of wolf body language and beginning to explore a variety of social relationships. But the pups presumably are not aware of this. They are simply rollicking with energy and the newfound enjoyment of one another's company. No matter how old they get, they will not lose these qualities. A wolf is never too old to play.

FACING PAGE: *Too young to leave the protection of the den, this brood of pups enjoy the warmth and watchfulness of their caregiver. Despite the adults' solicitude, about half of all pups die during their first year.* DANIEL J. COX

With its littermates close behind, a wolf pup emerges from the den into the pleasures of springtime. DANIEL J. COX

Wild Lives 65

Throughout the summer, the den provides a hub for the pack's activities. Each evening, the grownups go off to hunt, sometimes all together, sometimes alone or in small groups. Often the mother or a baby sitter remains at the den. By mid-morning, the hunters have returned, ready to spend a long dozy day; but before settling down to rest, each new arrival will likely be set upon by an eager mob of pups, who bite, lick and nudge insistently at the adult's mouth. This is their way of begging for food, and it may stimulate the grownup to regurgitate a heap of half-digested meat. While the pups gobble down their feast, the adults can enjoy a few moments of peace.

FACING PAGE: *Wolves nurse their pups for one or two months, before weaning them onto a diet of half-digested meat.* VICTORIA HURST, FIRST LIGHT

WHO'S HELPING WHOM?

Biologists are intrigued by the involvement of subordinate pack members as helpers in the care of the pups. According to evolutionary theory, the sole objective of an organism's life is to be the parent, grandparent and great-great-grandparent of as many descendants as possible. In this way, an individual ensures that its own personal genetic material is well represented in the future stock of the species. In the "struggle for survival," this is what counts—the survival of your genes into succeeding generations where they can continue to influence the course of evolution. So why would a wolf that had been forcibly prevented from producing its own offspring stick around to assist with rearing its oppressor's pups?

As we have seen, a wolf pack is basically a family. Although strangers may be admitted from time to time, most of the nonbreeding wolves who help at the den are daughters and sons of the breeding pair. More specifically, they are daughters and sons who have decided not to head out on their own but instead have chosen to remain with their parents, at least for the time being. Different wolves adopt different reproductive strategies. As yearlings, most of them make brief exploratory trips into the big wide world outside their home territory. Some of them disperse, never to be seen in the neighbourhood again. Indeed they may wander over many hundreds of kilometres in their search for a suitable mate and a vacant territory on which to establish their own pack. (This explains how wolves from Canada have been able to recolonize the northwestern states.) But other individuals decide to stay with their parents for a year or two, or even for a lifetime. Some of these "biders" are ambitious to advance in the sexual hierarchy and actively pursue the high social status that may permit them to become breeders. But others seem content to serve as nursemaids to offspring borne by other animals.

Although this behaviour may appear self-sacrificing, helping is also of benefit to the helpers. In fact, some biologists believe that many helpers are actually dependants. Still young and inexperienced, they may hang around the den in order to share in the hunting success of their parents and to beg for regurgitated treats from other pack members. Do helpers generally take more than they contribute? This question has not been clearly answered.

But let us assume that appearances hold, and it turns out that helpers really are helpful. A rationale for their behaviour can then be found in evolutionary theory. From a genetic point of view, an individual has the same degree of relationship to a sibling as to its own offspring. So a wolf that helps care for its younger siblings is also helping to

FACING PAGE: *A tolerant wolf mother allows herself to be mauled by three of her offspring. Pups are catered to by all the adults in the pack.* ART WOLFE

OVERLEAF: *Why walk if you can run? All head and feet, this dashing young pup is about three months old.* DANIEL J. COX

Wild Lives 69

ensure the survival of its own genes. Similarly, in cases of communal denning—a relatively rare occurrence in which a subordinate female bears young and then brings them to the alpha's den to spend their infancy—both females have a genetic stake in the other's progeny.

One way or another, wolf pups receive the devoted care not only of their parents but also of sisters, brothers, uncles, aunts and, occasionally, grandparents. Sometime in the first couple of months, the whole family may relocate to a new densite, with the youngsters transported, one by one, in the jaws of their mother. Then, when they are about eight or ten weeks old, too big and rambunctious for a burrow, the family relocates to an open-air home, or rendezvous site. This is an area of about a thousand square metres where the youngsters play and to which the adults return each day. A succession of similar meeting places is used till about September, when the yearly cycle of breeding and birth begins again.

FACING PAGE: *Abandoning its playthings for a while, a wolf pup dozes at the mouth of its den.*
DANIEL J. COX

Chapter 3 **THE HUNTERS AND THE HUNTED**

The first spring and summer of a young wolf's life pass in frolic and dependency, but with fall comes a crucial initiation into adulthood, as the pups join in the hunt. Pursuing large ungulates, armed with nothing but your teeth, is a dangerous and exacting occupation. The youngsters have much to learn. The first stage in their apprenticeship has been pouncing on mice and bugs back at the den and rendezvous site; the second stage will be watching the adults.

In his book *The Muskoxen of Polar Bear Pass*, David R. Gray tells of a wintery September day when he and a group of colleagues watched six wolves, including two pups, trot towards a herd of twelve muskoxen—towards massive, swinging horns and heavy, slashing front hooves backed by an average body weight of more than 300 kilograms (700 pounds). "Travelling in single file, the wolves approached to within about a hundred metres of the herd, which grouped, then separated. As it shifted around, one wolf lay down as two others circled the milling herd." Most of the muskoxen turned and fled, but the dominant bull faced his attackers. A wolf rushed at him, and the herd returned to stand together, shoulder to shoulder, in a defensive phalanx.

By now, several adult wolves were running loops around the closely grouped herd, while the pups stood quietly on the sidelines. Then two huge muskoxen lunged at one of the adult wolves. The adult backed off for a moment, then boldly renewed its attack, but the youngsters sped away with their tails between their legs. Whenever a muskox charged out at a wolf, another wolf rushed in and tried to cut it out of the herd, but the muskox always quickly regrouped in formation. Four minutes after the attack began, the wolves gave up and went to join the pups. "The herd remained grouped tightly together as all the wolves lay down [to rest]."

In many ways, this was a typical wolf hunt: dramatic yet inconclusive, coordinated yet far from rigidly disciplined. Each wolf took advantage of opportunities created by another's attack, as together they attempted to isolate a muskox from the protection of

FACING PAGE: *Acutely aware of every sound and scent (many of them beyond the reach of human senses), a wolf constantly scans its surroundings for information. To live by the hunt calls not only for physical strength and skill but also for a keen intelligence.* GLEN AND REBECCA GRAMBO

OVERLEAF: *To stay in good health, each wolf requires the equivalent of five to eight moose, or fifteen to eighteen deer, per year. With luck, an individual may survive for ten to twelve years.* TOM WALKER

the group. On other occasions, wolves have been known to adopt even more elaborate strategies that imply an ability not just for quick response but also for forethought. For example, one wolf may act as a decoy, by attacking and dashing around, while the rest of the pack moves in unnoticed to catch the prey off guard. Or sometimes one or two wolves run beyond their quarry and hide, out of sight. When the rest of the pack sets the prey in motion, this advance guard waits in ambush to attack. Once a kill is made, everyone shares in it.

When humans carry out coordinated strategies, their actions are usually the result of formal planning. But wolves cannot hold councils and talk their way to a consensus. Instead, each individual must decide for itself how to react, selecting from among its innate and learned hunting behaviours, and reacting to specific circumstances. What is the lie of the land? How is the prey responding? What actions have the other wolves, especially the high-ranking leaders, begun to take? We do not know how wolves make these quick and complex choices without the benefit of language, but we know they do it.

Obviously, a hunt requires focus, concentration, commitment. Yet it is not uncommon for wolves to break off for a short period of observation or rest ("one wolf lay down as two others circled the milling herd"), or to give up the attempt altogether even when it seems to a human observer that the predators still have a chance of success. Were Gray's wolves not hungry enough to press the attack (they did have a carcass nearby), or could they sense that it would be a waste of energy to proceed? Just because wolves want to kill an animal does not mean they will be able to. After all, they and their prey have evolved together, and in response to one another, for countless generations. Every advance in the wolves' ability to kill has been offset by an advance in their prey's ability to stay alive.

Travelling single-file, a pack of wolves sweeps through deep snow. No one knows how wolves decide where to travel in search of prey. Yet somehow, the animals make effective choices and pursue them with conviction. DANIEL J. COX

Although they also prey on smaller animals (notably beavers), wolves rely primarily on large ungulates such as mule and white-tail deer, elk, moose, caribou and, in this case, Dall's sheep. Wolf kills are an important source of winter protein for dozens of species of mammals and birds, including magpies.

THOMAS MANGELSEN

NATURAL BALANCE

The contest between predator and prey is an even match. Muskoxen have the advantage of their circular defence formation—rumps in the centre, heads towards the attacker, so that their flanks are protected and their weapons deployed. Caribou are protected by their erratic migrations, which make them hard to find, and by their sociability (it is difficult to make a kill in the midst of a stampeding herd). They and other members of the deer family have also acquired the ability to run a little faster than their enemies. Mountain goats, for their part, are able to escape up sheer cliff sides, where predators cannot trail them. Wolves have been one of the principal forces directing the evolution of these and other species, including moose, elk, bison and mountain sheep. These animals—the wolves' preferred prey—are specifically equipped to avoid wolf attacks. As the poet Robinson Jeffers once phrased it, "What but the wolf's tooth whittled so fine / The fleet limbs of the antelope?"

So it is not surprising that wolves are often unable to kill prey that is in prime condition. To be more accurate, they frequently do not bother to try. Biologists believe that wolves evaluate their prey for weaknesses that will permit an easy kill. In the case of caribou, they may test a herd by chasing it for a few minutes. If the prey stay bunched together and hurry nimbly away, the wolves immediately lose interest; but let one stumble or lag behind, and the wolves are quick to seize the advantage. Perhaps the brief attack on the muskoxen was just such a test. Since the animals all appeared strong, the wolves gave up. In general, that is the way most wolf hunts end. A kill is made only about one time in ten.

What are the factors that put an ungulate in this unlucky percentage? Perhaps it has an infectious disease or a severe infestation of parasites, or maybe it is hampered by injuries or age. Perhaps it is genetically inferior. Or it could be that the ungulate population has outgrown its range and the individual has been unable to get enough food. In all these circumstances, it seems possible that wolves may unwittingly benefit their prey species by culling out the sick and the weak and helping to keep the population in check. If inferior and unproductive animals are removed, then there will be more food for healthy, well-adapted animals and their young.

A case in point comes from Isle Royale in Lake Superior, where moose populations plummeted in the 1940s because of overpopulation and overbrowsing. But after a small population of wolves established itself on the island late in that decade, moose gradually increased to about six hundred in 1960 and fifteen hundred in 1970. David Mech, who

FACING PAGE: *A wolf strolls across the top of Brooks Falls, in Katmai National Park, Alaska, looking for fish. Wolves have been known to catch as many as five fish in fifteen minutes.* JOHNNY JOHNSON

Isle Royale is the simplest possible ecosystem, with one large carnivore (the wolf) and one ungulate (the moose). Elsewhere, predator-prey systems are generally more complex, as wolves, coyotes, mountain lions, grizzlies and other predators compete for a share of various deer species. DANIEL J. COX

studied the animals throughout that period, concluded that the wolves were removing mostly aged and inferior animals. Although the predators were also killing young calves, they were obviously not overtaxing the moose, whose reproductive capabilities (like those of all ungulates) had a built-in allowance for such losses. These findings seemed to support the time-honoured belief that predator and prey maintain a finely tuned balance—a gentle rhythm of reciprocal ups and downs that never swings far from equilibrium. By and large, this generalization is still thought to hold true.

FACING PAGE: *As David Mech concluded in 1970, the importance of wolves in maintaining "the stability of natural communities" is reason enough to be concerned for their survival. But it is not the only reason.* DANIEL J. COX

With its tail tucked between its legs, a wolf flees from a charging grizzly bear. Although the grizzly was the victor in this case, the two species are evenly matched, and confrontations (over ownership of a carcass, for example) may be won by either party. RICH KIRCHNER

CRASHES AND CHAOS

But there are exceptions to the rule of "balance" in predator-prey systems. Back on Isle Royale in the early 1970s, the land and the animals suffered through a series of brutal winters. Mired in deep snow, half-starved and weak, adult and calf moose both became easy pickings for a large and energetic population of wolves. Moose numbers crashed—down to half by the middle of the decade. But wolf numbers continued to rise, achieving a threefold increase by 1980. Apparently, the calves that had grown up during hard times remained vulnerable to predation throughout their lifetimes, so the wolves continued to feast even after the moose had tottered into decline. Eventually, through a gruesome combination of malnutrition, social strife and disease, the wolves were also reduced from a triumphant high of fifty to a remnant of fourteen individuals. Since then, although moose populations have recovered fully, the fortunes of the wolves have been uncertain. For reasons that remain obscure (inbreeding? illness?), they have rebounded and died off, rebounded and died off, and rebounded again, in a wavering struggle against extinction.

Obviously, the dance of predator with prey is not always elegant and even-tempered. Predator and prey do not always stay neatly "in balance." Take the case of the Spatsizi caribou herd in northern British Columbia. In the late seventies, biologists became aware that the caribou were declining drastically because they were producing very few calves. What was going on? Were the females failing to get pregnant? No, that couldn't be the problem because in May almost 90 per cent of them had large udders, a sure sign that they were going to give birth. Were the newborns dying in spring storms? No, when the investigators scrambled up the mountains after the caribou in June, they found lots of big, healthy calves. Three-quarters of the cows had young. But by early July, the calves were virtually gone. They had been eaten by grizzlies, wolverines—and wolves. Although moose were also available in the area, the fresh wolf scats collected on the calving grounds contained one hundred per cent caribou.

In this case, the decimation of the caribou herd had not brought about a reduction in the number of predators. For most of the year, the wolves could rely on moose, beaver and other prey to support the pups that kept their populations at moderately high levels. But in June, all these hungry canines turned their attention to the juicy delicacies on the caribou calving-ground. In the frenzied delight of easy hunting, they sometimes killed more than they could eat and so, together with other predators, quickly wiped out almost the entire season's "crop" of young caribou.

To some people, these facts may suggest that wolves are nasty, immoral animals who ought to show more decency and a better sense of consequences. But this, of course, is foolishness. Wolves are predators. Their "job" is killing to feed themselves and their offspring, and that is what we must expect them to do. Their impact on their prey is not limited by high-minded principles but by intricate natural processes. Under most circumstances, they do not become so plentiful that they gobble up everything in sight. Although wolf numbers rise and fall in keeping with their food supply, their ups and downs are tempered by stabilizing forces in their social life. Territoriality limits the number of packs that may occupy a certain area; social interactions regulate the number of births within each pack. While these processes don't put a ceiling on the population (as was once thought), they generally do prevent wolves from reproducing so fast that they outstrip their food supply. Thus, over the long term and over large areas, wolves and their prey both manage to get by.

Over the long term and over large areas. But in the short term and under specific local conditions, wolves may be capable of sending their prey, and sometimes themselves, into population declines, or at least of exacerbating such trends. Presumably, these downward turns are often the descending curves of self-correcting natural cycles, though we humans seldom have the patience to wait them out.

WOLVES AND POLITICS

It is within this haze of uncertainties that wildlife officials are challenged to make their decisions about wolf "management." And this is not the end of the difficulties, for there is another factor to be entered into the equation, itself surrounded by a fog of conflicting facts and feelings. This is the question of the human use of animals. If human hunters decide they have a right to "harvest" moose or caribou from a declining population, they will not necessarily rejoice at the presence of four-footed competitors. Why, the hunters may ask, should we wait through a long and uncertain natural cycle if we can introduce a measure of stability by curtailing wolves? Why let predators cream off the increase in a deer population if, by removing them for a while, we are able to boost the amount of prey for both humans and wolves in future years?

Our recent ancestors, as we know, found easy answers to these perplexities. They simply set about eradicating wolves: not limiting or "controlling" them, but wiping them out. Unhappily, there are still a few throwbacks eager to promote this course of action. One thinks, for example, of the gentlemen in southeastern Alberta who, in 1994, saw to the killing of more than forty wolves—about 75 per cent of a recovering population on the east slope of the Canadian Rockies. But most of us have had our fill of slaughter. We are becoming aware that other species, like ourselves, are creatures of the Earth. "Wolves, like all other wildlife, have a right to exist in a wild state," declares the manifesto on wolf conservation issued by the Wolf Specialist Group of the International Union for the Conservation of Nature. "This right is in no way related to their known value to mankind. Instead, it derives from the right of all living creatures to co-exist with [people] as part of natural ecosystems."

But if it is too brutal to claim everything for ourselves, it is unrealistic to insist that no wolf must ever be harmed again. Personally, I have never taken the life of anything bigger than a fish nor cuter than a mouse. When I find a bee or spider in my house, I carry it outdoors. But I have eaten many dead animals in my time, and I respect the people who raise and kill them on my behalf. If there are individual wolves that develop a tradition of killing livestock, it seems barely tolerable that those animals might be identified and shot. Provided that stock growers take proper care of their herds and flocks—by ensuring that lambs and calves are born under close supervision, reducing or eliminating their use of remote pastures, and removing carcasses from their land—then incidents of predation, and losses of wolves, will be very rare. Where wild prey is available, few wolves pay much attention to sheep and cattle.

Farmers and ranchers who meet high standards in their husbandry practices deserve to be compensated, at fair market value, when they do lose stock to wolves. The rest of us must be prepared to pay the price, either through our taxes or—in jurisdictions where governments are taking a principled stand against public governance—through private subscriptions. The Defenders of Wildlife, the Canadian Parks and Wilderness Association and other conservation groups in Canada and the U.S. have established funds, supported by donation, from which to make compensation payments. They have done so because asking livestock producers to bear the cost of wolf predation is more than unfair. It is also unwise. All the world needs is a legion of outraged folks, armed with a legitimate and impatient sense of grievance, who set their sights not only on wolves but also on legislation that fosters wolf recovery—the American Endangered Species Act, for example, and a proposed federal law in Canada.

This realization also influenced the recent decision to reintroduce wolves into Yellowstone National Park and northern Idaho. Wildlife officials there had the option of relying on the slow but almost sure process of natural recolonization, which they expected to succeed within about thirty years. If the wolves had reappeared of their own accord, they would automatically have been entitled to the full protection of the Endangered Species Act. Instead, twenty-nine animals from northern Alberta were airlifted into the area in 1995 (with more to follow in succeeding years) as an "experimental population," a designation that leaves wildlife technicians more latitude for dealing with wolves that are identified as "problems." This is not a heroic compromise—it puts the wolves in personal jeopardy—but it may be politically astute. The proof will be the long-term survival not only of a vigorous population of wolves but also of an adequately financed and legally sanctioned conservation strategy.

BEYOND SURVIVAL

The future well-being of wolves is not a question of biology. Of all the species that are currently in jeopardy around the world, few are as well-positioned by nature to make a recovery. Intelligent and versatile, they can adapt to reasonably high levels of human activity. As long as people refrain from shooting too many of them (which unfortunately seems too much to ask in many localities), wolves are relatively unaffected by logging, mining, farms, towns, and four-lane highways. Even when they do suffer heavy losses, they often rebound quite readily. Unlike most predators, they reproduce quickly, especially when their social order breaks down and liberated subordinates are free to bear young. Difficult to discourage, quick to bounce back, wolves are a zestful evolutionary force that, given a decent chance, will overcome most obstacles put in its path.

They have surmounted even the controversial "wolf control" programs recently carried out in Alaska and the Yukon. The killing of dozens or even hundreds of wolves in a circumscribed area, provided there are healthy populations all around to provide an influx of replacements, is not a threat to the species' overall survival. In fact, the reduction might even lead to a population surge, *if* biologists are right to think that depressed ungulate herds, given a temporary break from predators, will level out at higher levels than they held before. The bottom line in scientists' calculations is productivity, and the goal is to provide more of everything—more moose, more caribou, more wolves, more "game" for outfitters, more meat for subsistence hunters and more viewable wildlife for tourists and tour operators.

But the invisible cost of these hoped-for gains is the suffering of wolves—invisible, that is, until biologist Gordon Haber, working for the Alaska Wildlife Alliance in 1994, videotaped the death agony of "control" victims in Alaska. One young pup, trying to escape from a snare, had chewed through its right leg near the shoulder. When these images were made public, the wolf-kill was immediately suspended—but for how long? The likelihood is that wolf "control" will continue to be an attractive strategy for wildlife managers in regions where wolves are relatively plentiful. Hardened to suffering ("animals die horrible deaths all the time") and challenged to provide bountiful hunting for their human clientele, wildlife officers have few options. When an ungulate herd declines, they can restrict or even close human hunting for a time (and frequently do so), but they cannot correct last season's "overharvest" nor control the severity of the coming winter. There is only one button left to push, and it is marked "Kill Wolves."

Personally, I believe there are times when it is legitimate to shoot wolves in order to assist the recovery of ungulate herds. I would do it, for example, to protect a remnant population of woodland caribou from extinction. I would do it to benefit aboriginal subsistence hunters who were threatened with hardship. For me, the suffering of the wolves would be justified in these extreme circumstances, as we attempted to safeguard our diminishing stores of biological or cultural diversity. But it is obnoxious to kill large numbers of wolves, year after year, decade after decade, as part of the routine management of ungulate herds, even if the losses can theoretically be sustained. Surely we want more for wolves than a fugitive's tentative survival. Surely, after all the destruction we have inflicted on them, we are ready to grant the survivors a measure of peace.

Wolves have a right to more than mere survival as a species. They have a right to forests and plains and mountain valleys with a natural abundance of mule deer and caribou and moose. They have a right to safety and to space—large, connected tracts of wild country that can support large, flourishing populations of predators and prey. As much as possible, we should leave them alone to enjoy this legacy. And meanwhile, there is plenty for us to do. The legal and administrative measures that have protected wolves and other species for the past few decades are both fragile and fragmentary. Where they exist, they could be revoked with the stroke of a pen. Where they are lacking (as they are in Canada), they are often urgently needed. New strategies are also a pressing requirement—like the World Wildlife Fund's proposal to create conservation zones that would extend the boundaries of protection for large carnivores beyond the scraps of wilderness that have been reserved as parks. Such initiatives will need skilled nurturance if they are to survive the mean-spirited politics of the 1990s and beyond.

If they are to survive. It is late afternoon on the tundra in the valley of the wolves, and the air lies breathless and still. Since the pups vanished a few days ago, the adults also seem to have disappeared. There is no longer anything to keep them here. But now, a wisp of breeze drifts across the hillside and on it, for a moment, wafts the lingering song of a wolf. Across the gully we pick out the dominant male, his white coat glistening against the grey-green slope. His howling is cool and melancholy, and when it fades, the silence deepens.

The wolf settles behind a boulder to sleep. Half an hour creeps by. Then suddenly, he's on his feet, his tail wagging in joy. Another wolf has emerged out of nowhere to answer his call. A head appears alongside his, nudging his muzzle; a second mad tail joins in the enthusiasm of the greeting. Catching the spirit of the occasion, we watchers can't help but grin.

We humans are not alone on this planet. We are close kin to the lichens, the wind, the stars; we are closest of kin to wolves. Through them, we are reminded that we too are creatures of nature. Through their inspiration, perhaps we can yet find the will to act on behalf of our own vital interests. By caring for wolves, we care for ourselves, body and spirit.

FACING PAGE: *Wolves are keepers of the wild. They have a right to peace; we have a right to their company.* DENVER BRYAN

OVERLEAF: *Companions.*
ALAN AND SANDY CAREY

The Hunters and the Hunted 97

Giving voice. RICH KIRCHNER

100 **Wolves**

REFERENCES

The literature on wolves is vast, and this reference listing is necessarily selective. Items marked with an asterisk* are especially recommended for further reading.

The maps on page 8 are based on information from the European Wolf Network, the International Wolf Center, the Ontario Ministry of Natural Resources and the Ontario Trappers Association.

GENERAL

Brandenburg, Jim. *Brother Wolf: A Forgotten Promise.* Minocqua, Minn.: North Word, 1993.

* Carbyn, Ludwig N. "Gray Wolf and Red Wolf." In *Wild Furbearer Management and Conservation in North America,* M. Novak; G. A. Baker; M. E. Obbard; and B. Malloch; eds. 359–76. Toronto: Ontario Trappers Association and Ontario Ministry of Natural Resources, 1987.

Hall, Roberta L., and Henry S. Sharp, eds. *Wolf and Man: Evolution in Parallel.* New York: Academic Press, 1978.

Harrington, Fred H., and Paul C. Paquet, eds. *Wolves of the World: Perspectives on Behavior, Ecology, and Conservation.* Park Ridge, N. J.: Noyes Publications, 1982.

* Hummel, Monte, and Sherry Pettigrew. *Wild Hunters: Predators in Peril.* Toronto: Key Porter Books, 1991.

International Wolf Center. *Wolves of the High Arctic.* Photographs by L. David Mech. Stillwater, Minn.: Voyageur Press, 1992.

* Mech, L. David. *The Arctic Wolf: Living with the Pack.* Stillwater, Minnesota: Voyageur Press, 1988.

* ———. *The Wolf: The Ecology and Behavior of an Endangered Species.* Garden City, N.Y.: American Museum of Natural History and Natural History Press, 1970.

Wolves and Humans 2000: A Global Perspective for Managing Conflict. Program and abstracts from an international symposium. University of Minnesota Duluth and International Wolf Center, 1995.

Zimen, Erik. *The Wolf: His Place in the Natural World.* London: Souvenir Press, 1981.

Chapter 1 **WOLF MAGIC**

Bernard, Daniel. *L'homme et le loup.* Paris: Éditions Libre Expression, 1981.

Carbyn, Ludwig N. "Canada's 50,000 wolves." *International Wolf* 4, no. 4 (1994): 3–8.

———. "Wolf population fluctuations in Jasper National Park, Alberta, Canada." *Biological Conservation* 6 (1974): 94–101.

———. *Wolves in Canada and Alaska.* Canadian Wildlife Service Report Series No. 25, 1983.

Heard, Douglas C. *Historical and Present Status of Wolves in the Northwest Territories.* Northwest Territories Renewable Resources Information Series Report No. 4, 1984.

Henriksen, Georg. *Hunters in the Barrens: The Naskapi on the Edge of the White Man's World.* St. John's: Memorial University of Newfoundland, 1973.

Jenness, Stuart E. "Arctic wolf attacks scientist: a unique Canadian incident." *Arctic* 38 (1985): 129–32.

Linderman, Frank B. *Plenty-Coups: Chief of the Crows.* Lincoln: University of Nebraska Press, 1962.

* Lopez, Barry Holstun. *Of Wolves and Men.* New York: Charles Scribner's Sons, 1978.

Mowat, Farley. *Never Cry Wolf.* Toronto: Seal Books, 1983.

Neumann, Erich. *The Great Mother: An Analysis of the Archetype.* Princeton, N.J.: Princeton University Press, 1963.

Okarma, Henryk. "Status and management of the wolf in Poland." *Biological Conservation* 66 (1993): 153–58.

Promberger, Christoph; Wolf Schroder; and Doris Hofer. "The European Wolf Network: coordinating national conservation efforts to a European campaign." In *Wolves and Humans 2000: A Global Perspective for Managing Conflict.* Program and abstracts from an international symposium. University of Minnesota Duluth and International Wolf Center, 1995.

Randi, E.; V. Lucchini; and F. Francisci. "Allozyme variability in the Italian wolf (*Canis lupus*) population." *Heredity* 71 (1993): 516-22.

Ray, Dorothy Jean. *Eskimo Masks: Art and Ceremony.* Toronto: McClelland and Stewart, 1967.

Schmidt, Joel. *Larousse Greek and Roman Mythology.* New York: McGraw-Hill, 1980.

Seton, Ernest Thompson. *Lives of Game Animals.* Boston: C.T. Branford, 1953 [1909].

Walker, Barbara G. *The Woman's Encyclopedia of Myths and Secrets.* San Francisco: Harper and Row, 1983.

Chapter 2 **WILD LIVES**

Bromley, Robert G. "Fishing behaviour of a wolf on the Taltson River, Northwest Territories." *Canadian Field-Naturalist* 87 (1973): 301–303.

Carbyn, Ludwig N. "Territory displacement in a wolf population with abundant prey." *Journal of Mammalogy* 62 (1981): 193–95.

Crisler, Lois. *Arctic Wild.* New York: Harper and Brothers, 1958.

Derix, Ruud; Jan Van Hooff; Hans De Vries; and Joep Wensing. "Male and female mating competition in wolves: female suppression vs. male intervention." *Behaviour* 127 (1993): 141–71.

Harrington, Fred H. "Urine-marking and caching behaviour in the wolf." *Behaviour* 76 (1981): 280–88.

Harrington, Fred H.; L. David Mech; and Steven H. Fritts. "Pack size and wolf pup survival: their relationship under varying ecological conditions." *Behavioral Ecology and Sociobiology* 13 (1983): 19–26.

Joslin, Paul W. B. "Movements and home sites of timber wolves in Algonquin Park." *American Zoologist* 7 (1967): 279–88.

Klinghammer, Erich, ed. *The Behavior and Ecology of Wolves.* New York: Garlan STPM Press, 1979.

Kuyt, E. "Movements of young wolves in the Northwest Territories of Canada." *Journal of Mammalogy* 43 (1962): 270–71.

Lehman, Niles; Peter Clarkson; L. David Mech; Thomas J. Meier; and Robert K. Wayne. "A study of the genetic relationships within and among wolf packs using DNA fingerprinting and mitochondrial DNA." *Behavioral Ecology and Sociobiology* 30 (1992): 83–94.

Mech, L. David. "Buffer zones of territories of gray wolves as regions of intraspecific strife." *Journal of Mammalogy* 75 (1994): 199–202.

———. "Wolf-pack buffer zones as prey reservoirs." *Science* 198 (1977): 320–21.

* Murie, Adolph. *The Wolves of Mount McKinley.* Fauna of the National Parks of the United States, Fauna Series No. 5, 1971 [1941].

Packard, Jane M., and L. David Mech. "Population Regulation in Wolves." In *Biosocial Mechanisms of Population Regulation*, M. N. Cohen, et al.; eds. 135–50. New Haven: Yale University Press, 1980.

Peterson, Rolf O. *Wolf Ecology and Prey Relationships on Isle Royale.* National Park Service Scientific Monograph Series 11, 1977.

Rabb, George B.; Jerome H. Woolpy; and Benson E. Ginsburg. "Social relationships in a group of captive wolves." *American Zoologist* 7 (1967): 305–11.

Savage, Arthur, and Candace Savage. *Wild Mammals of Western Canada.* Saskatoon, Sask: Western Producer Prairie Books, 1981.

Schenkel, Rudolf. "Submission: its features and function in the wolf and dog." *American Zoologist* 7 (1967): 319–20.

Theberge, John B. *Wolves and Wilderness.* Toronto: Dent, 1975.

Theberge, John B., and Bruce J. Falls. "Howling as a means of communication in timber wolves." *American Zoologist* 7 (1967): 331–38.

Woolpy, Jerome H., and Benson E. Ginsburg. "Wolf socialization: a study of temperament in a wild social species." *American Zoologist* 7 (1967): 357–63.

Chapter 3 **THE HUNTERS AND THE HUNTED**

Alvistur, Jose. "Alaska's official wolf slaughter suspended." *Colorado Wolf Tracks* 4, no. 4 (1995): 6.

Ballard, Warren B.; Jackson S. Whitman; and Craig L. Gardner. "Ecology of an exploited wolf population in south-central Alaska." *Wildlife Monographs* 98, 1987.

Bergerud, A. T.; W. Wyett; and B. Snider. "The role of wolf predation in limiting a moose population." *Journal of Wildlife Management* 47 (1983): 977–88.

* Boutin, Stan. "Predation and moose population dynamics: a critique." *Journal of Wildlife Management* 56 (1992): 116–127.

Carbyn, Ludwig N. "Management of non-endangered wolf populations in Canada." *Acta Zool. Fennica* 174 (1983): 239–43.

———. "Wolf predation on elk in Riding Mountain National Park, Manitoba." *Journal of Wildlife Management* 47 (1983): 963–76.

Carbyn, L. N.; S. M. Oosenbrug; and D. W. Anions. *Wolves, Bison and the Dynamics Related to the Peace-Athabasca Delta in Canada's Wood Buffalo National Park.* Canadian Circumpolar Research Institute Research Series Number 4, 1993.

Decker, Daniel J., and Tommy L. Brown. "How animal rightists view the 'wildlife management-hunting system.'" *Wildlife Society Bulletin* 15 (1987): 599–602.

Fritts, Steven H., and Ludwig N. Carbyn. "Population viability, nature reserves, and the outlook for gray wolf conservation in North America." *Restoration Ecology* 3 (1995): 26–38.

Fritts, Steven H.; William J. Paul; and L. David Mech. "Can relocated wolves survive?" *Wildlife Society Bulletin* 13 (1985): 459–63.

Fuller, Todd K. *Guidelines for Gray Wolf Management in the Northern Great Lakes Region.* Ely, Minn.: International Wolf Center, 1995.

Gray, David R. *The Muskoxen of Polar Bear Pass.* Toronto: Fitzhenry and Whiteside, 1987.

Haber, Gordon C. "The balancing act of moose and wolves." *Natural History* 89, no. 10 (1980): 38–51.

"He Said, We Said." *Nature Canada* 22, no. 4 (1993): 28–29.

Lidle, Janet, ed. *Wolf!* (An independent quarterly newsletter, committed to the survival of the wolf in the wild and its welfare in captivity.) Vol. 4, no. 3 (1986); vol. 5, no.1–4 (1987).

Marty, Sid. "A killing season in the Rockies." *Canadian Geographic* 115, no. 3 (1995): 17.

Mech, L. David. *The Wolves of Isle Royale.* Fauna of the National Parks of the United States, Fauna Series 7, 1966.

Messier, François. "Ungulate population models with predation: a case study with the North American moose." *Ecology* 75 (1994): 478–88.

Messier, François, and Michel Crete. "Moose-wolf dynamics and the natural regulation of moose populations." *Oecologia* 65 (1985): 503–12.

Miller, D. R. "Observations of wolf predation on barren ground caribou in winter." *First International Reindeer and Caribou Symposium.* Biological Papers of the University of Alaska, Special Report No. 1, 1975, pp. 209–20.

Miller, Frank L.; Anne Gunn; and Eric Broughton. "Surplus killing as exemplified by wolf predation on newborn caribou." *Canadian Journal of Zoology* 63 (1985): 295–300.

Nelson, Michael E., and L. David Mech. "Observation of a wolf killed by a deer." *Journal of Mammalogy* 66 (1985): 187–88.

Obee, Bruce. "Wolves of British Columbia: predator or prey?" *Wildlife Review* (summer, 1984): 5–25.

Pimlott, Douglas H. "Wolf control in Canada." Reprinted from *Canadian Audubon Magazine* by the Canadian Wildlife Service, 1961.

Ramsay, M. A., and D. R. Seip, eds. "Symposium on wolf predation." Simon Fraser University, December 1, 1978.

Seip, Dale R. "Factors limiting woodland caribou populations and their interrelationships with wolves and moose in southeastern British Columbia." *Canadian Journal of Zoology* 70 (1992): 1494–1503.

Theberge, John B., and David A. Gauthier. "Models of wolf-ungulate relationships: when is wolf control justified?" *Wildlife Society Bulletin* 13 (1985): 449–58.

Thurber, Joanne M., and Rolf O. Peterson. "Effects of population density and pack size on the foraging ecology of gray wolves." *Journal of Mammalogy* 74 (1993): 879–89.

Thurber, Joanne M.; Rolf O. Peterson; Thomas D. Drummer; and Scott A. Thomasma. "Gray wolf response to refuge boundaries and roads in Alaska." *Wildlife Society Bulletin* 22 (1994): 61–68.

LIVESTOCK COMPENSATION PROGRAMS

For more information on programs that compensate livestock producers for losses to wolves and other large predators, please contact the organizations listed below.

Portions of the western United States are covered by

The Defenders of Wildlife
1534 Mansfield Avenue
Missoula, Montana 59801

A program for southwestern Alberta has been established through the cooperation of several organizations, including

Waterton Natural History Association
Box 145
Waterton, Alberta T0K 2M0

Canadian Parks and Wilderness Society
Box 608, Sub P.O. Box 91
University of Calgary
Calgary, Alberta T2N 1N4

Both the Canadian and American programs rely on donations for their support, and contributions are always welcome.

INDEX